Growing up in Wilmington, Delaware, I eagerly looked forward to the Passover holiday. My Uncle Jack led the Seder. He would mumble every word of the service from his Haggadah, which was different from everyone else's, so that from the start we were all hopelessly lost. Sitting next to him was my Aunt Esther, who was always angry and banging on the table because we weren't listening and not acting responsibly. Of course, this just made my other aunts and uncles laugh and talk even louder.

My sister, my cousins and I were busy making juvenile noises and jokes while my mother desperately tried to keep the Seder on track. Since my father had passed away, she felt she had to preserve these family gatherings with all the traditions. In the kitchen were several of the women who had a half-dozen huge pots steaming and kept yelling, "Are you people done with the *brochos* yet?"

All in all, it was a great dinner celebration but I had only the vaguest notion of what it was about.

My wife, Liora, growing up on kibbutz had a totally different Passover experience. The kibbutz Seder was a huge event held in the communal dining hall with hundreds of members and their guests. They were dressed in new embroidered white shirts and dresses. Teenage girls danced and a children's choir sang. Their Haggadah and ceremony were closely connected to the land, the renewal of spring and the coming of the first harvest.

With our children, Liora and I wanted to make a Seder that blended the best of both our Passover celebrations. We searched for a suitable Haggadah but couldn't find one that was a good fit, so we decided to make our own. We have followed the traditional structure but clarified the rituals and the story so that it flows coherently from beginning to end. We've shortened the explanations and condensed the prayers without losing their essential meaning. By making the Haggadah less confusing and more entertaining, everyone – from the wise one who knows the history and observes the Passover rituals to the newcomer "who doesn't even know how to ask" – can fully participate. Even Aunt Esther wouldn't complain – maybe. Have a joyous Passover.

Richard and Liora Codor

Richard Codor's

JOYOUS HAGGADAH

THE ILLUMINATED STORY OF PASSOVER

As told by

Richard and Liora Codor

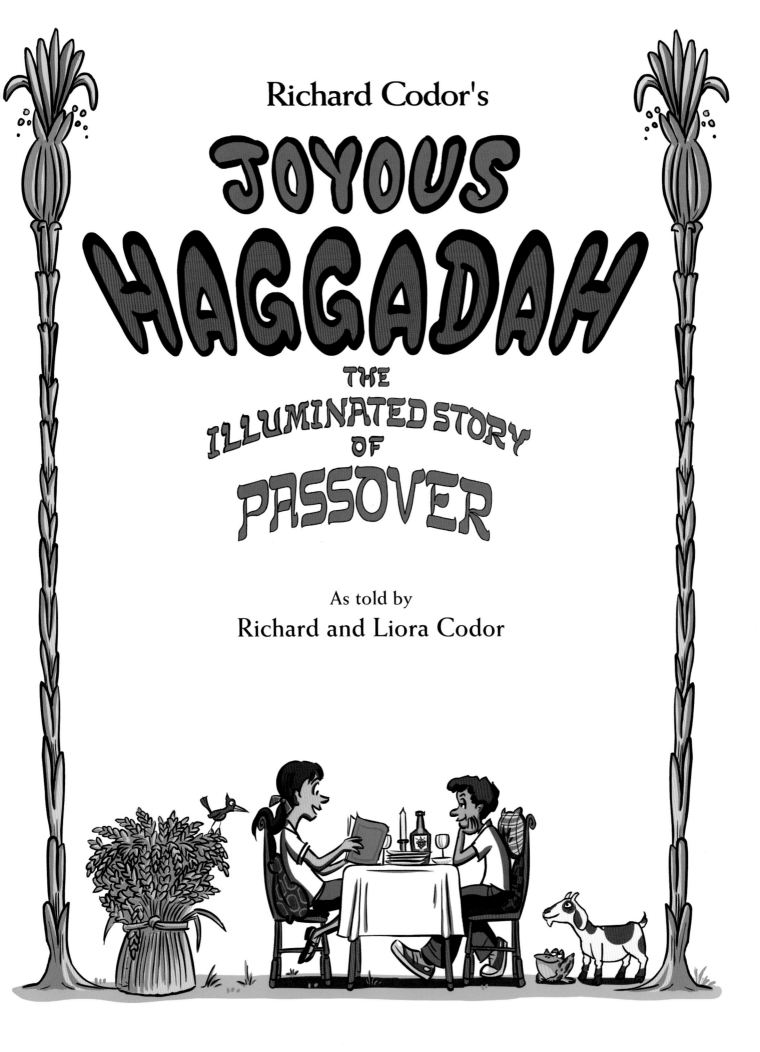

In memory of my sister, Janet

Graphic design by Jo Ellingson

Edited by Zelda Shluker

Hebrew type by Rachel Fyman

Special thanks for additional editorial help
to Beverly Rubman
and to Mark Goldfus for his stick figures.

Richard Codor's Joyous Haggadah
Copyright© 2008, 2013 by Richard Codor
1st Edition 2008,
2nd Printing 2009
3rd Printing 2013
4th Printing 2014
5th Printing 2016

ISBN-13: 978-0-9799218-0-3
ISBN-10: 0-9799218-0-5
Library of Congress Control Number: 2007907471

Loose Line Productions, Inc.

Published by Loose Line Productions, Inc.
www.joyoushaggadah.net

For orders contact:
Haggadahs-R-Us
Joe Buchwald Gelles
Toll-free 877-308-4175
jbgelles@gmail.com
www.haggadahsrus.com

Printed in Malaysia

The Order of the Passover Seder

Wine Blessing / *Kadesh* קַדֵּשׁ

Washing Hands / *U-Rechatz* וּרְחַץ

Parsley / *Karpas* כַּרְפַּס

Dividing the Matzah / *Yachatz* יַחַץ

Telling the Story / *Maggid* מַגִּיד

Washing Hands / *Rochtzah* רָחְצָה

Blessing for Matzah / *Motzi Matzah* מוֹצִיא מַצָּה

Bitter Herbs / *Maror* מָרוֹר

Sandwich / *Korekh* כּוֹרֵךְ

Festive Meal / *Shulchan Orekh* שֻׁלְחָן עוֹרֵךְ

Hidden Dessert / *Tzafun* צָפוּן

Blessing after Meal / *Barekh* בָּרֵךְ

Praising God / *Hallel* הַלֵּל

Conclusion / *Nirtzah* נִרְצָה

Wine Blessing / *Kadesh*

קַדֵּשׁ

Welcome to the Haggadah, which means the "Telling." The Telling and everything else tonight is done in a special order or "Seder." We begin with the Kadesh, the traditional blessing of the wine, the first of four cups we'll drink tonight. Raise your glass with your right hand and say:

בָּרוּךְ אַתָּה יְיָ, אֱלֹהֵינוּ מֶלֶךְ הָעוֹלָם,
בּוֹרֵא פְּרִי הַגָּפֶן.

Barukh Ata Adonai, Eloheinu Melekh ha-olam, borei pri ha-gaffen.

Blessed are You, our God, Ruler of the Universe, Creator of the fruit of the vine.

Drink and turn the page…

Washing Hands / *U-Rechatz*
וּרְחַץ

Next, wash your hands in the little bowls on the
table. There's no blessing but it's a nice, clean tradition.

Parsley / *Karpas*
כַּרְפַּס

The Seder leader passes around sprigs
of parsley that we dip into a bowl of salted
water. This isn't just another healthy
vegetable that you have to eat but a
reminder of the Israelite slaves' bitter tears mixed
with the renewed hope of spring and freedom.

בָּרוּךְ אַתָּה יְיָ, אֱלֹהֵינוּ מֶלֶךְ הָעוֹלָם, בּוֹרֵא פְּרִי הָאֲדָמָה.

Barukh Ata Adonai, Eloheinu Melekh ha-olam, borei pri ha-adamah.

Blessed are You, our God, Ruler of the Universe,
Creator of the fruit of the earth.

Dividing the Matzah / *Yachatz*
יַחַץ

On the table are three covered matzahs. They represent
the priestly Kohanim, the Levites and the rest of the Israelite tribes.
Tonight, all of us are united with our ancestral matzah under
one roof. The leader of the Seder breaks off a large piece of the middle
matzah and wraps it in a white napkin and hides it (no peeking).
This is the *Afikoman*. After the meal, your mission
is to find it and receive your just reward.

Near the head of the table is the Seder Plate.

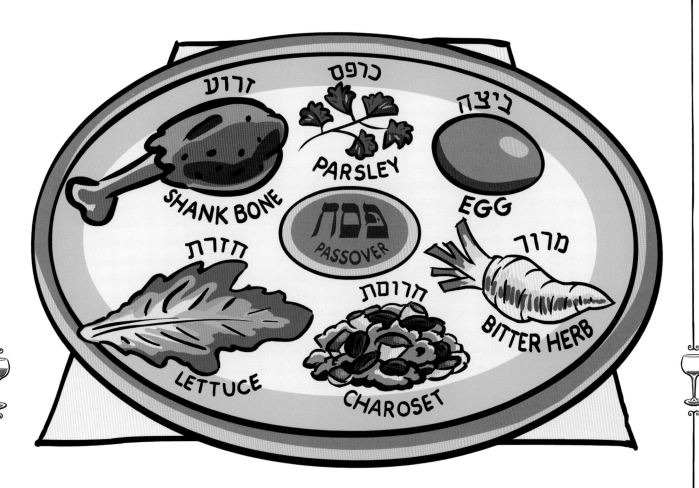

זרוע
SHANK BONE

כרפס
PARSLEY

ביצה
EGG

חזרת
LETTUCE

פסח
PASSOVER

מרור
BITTER HERB

חרוסת
CHAROSET

On the plate are other foods with special
meaning for the Seder but more about them later.
For now, just look and don't touch.

Next to the Seder Plate
is a big wine goblet filled to the brim.
It's for a mysterious, white bearded
stranger who comes in through the partly
opened front door. Whether you see him
or not, all guests, real or invisible,
are welcome to this festive dinner.

Telling the Story / *Maggid*
מַגִּיד

By now, you're probably confused, wondering what this is all about. Don't despair. You're not alone. At this point, the youngest reader among us takes over and asks the following questions. We join in, saying them as if for the first time:

THE FOUR QUESTIONS

Mah nishtanah ha-lailah ha-zeh mi-kol ha-leilot?

Why is this night different from all other nights?

1) She-bekhol ha-leilot anu okhlin
chameitz u-matzah, ha-lailah ha-zeh kuloh matzah.

On all other nights during the year we eat either bread or matzah, but on this night we eat only matzah.

2) She-bekhol ha-leilot anu okhlin
she'ar yerakot, ha-lailah ha-zeh maror.

On all other nights we eat all kinds of herbs, but on this night we eat only bitter herbs.

3) She-bekhol ha-leilot ein anu mat'bilin
afilu pa'am echat, ha-lailah ha-zeh shetei fe'amim.

On all other nights we do not dip our herbs even once, but on this night we dip them twice.

4) She-bekhol ha-leilot anu okhlin bein
yosh'vin u-vein mesubin, ha-lailah ha-zeh kulanu mesubin.

On all other nights we eat either sitting or reclining, but on this night we all eat reclining.

מַה נִּשְׁתַּנָּה הַלַּיְלָה הַזֶּה מִכָּל הַלֵּילוֹת?

1) שֶׁבְּכָל הַלֵּילוֹת אָנוּ אוֹכְלִין חָמֵץ וּמַצָּה,
הַלַּיְלָה הַזֶּה כֻּלּוֹ מַצָּה.

2) שֶׁבְּכָל הַלֵּילוֹת אָנוּ אוֹכְלִין שְׁאָר יְרָקוֹת,
הַלַּיְלָה הַזֶּה מָרוֹר.

3) שֶׁבְּכָל הַלֵּילוֹת אֵין אָנוּ מַטְבִּילִין אֲפִילוּ
פַּעַם אֶחָת, הַלַּיְלָה הַזֶּה שְׁתֵּי פְעָמִים.

4) שֶׁבְּכָל הַלֵּילוֹת אָנוּ אוֹכְלִין בֵּין יוֹשְׁבִין
וּבֵין מְסֻבִּין, הַלַּיְלָה הַזֶּה כֻּלָּנוּ מְסֻבִּין.

11

Why is this night different than all other nights? On every other night we can eat any bread, roll, pita or bagel. But on this night we eat only matzah. On any other night there are the usual vegetables to choose from. Tonight, there's horseradish, red and white, hot and hotter.

What other night do you dip parsley or celery or lettuce in salted water - *twice*? Every night you're told, "Don't slouch. Sit up straight." But tonight everyone is all dressed up and happily relaxed in pillow-stuffed chairs.

For thousands of years, on this same night Jews of every size, shape and color, wherever they lived, ask those same Four Questions, and the answer is: This is the Passover Seder. In every generation, we celebrate this night as if *we* are the slaves throwing off Pharaoh's oppressive chains and marching out of Egypt to freedom.

onight, we are all like children, curious about what happened so long ago. To understand those events you need the right answers, and to get the right answers you need to ask the right questions. The Haggadah tells of four very different children who are taught in four very different ways.

חָכָם

The Wise Child / *Chakham*

The wise son or daughter probably knows the story backward and forward. He or she always want to know more. So you teach them everything you know about Passover down to the last little detail. Maybe you'll learn something new, too.

שָׁעָ

The Wicked Child / *Rasha*

The wicked child says, "What's in it for me? Who cares?" A child with that attitude would miss the last donkey out of Egypt and still be Pharaoh's slave today.

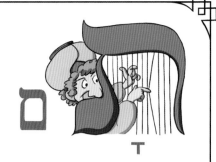

The Simple Child / *Tam*

The simple child may be smarter than he looks, but you have to spell out everything for him. Just remind him that a strong hand brought us out of Egypt and we have no intention of going back. Now we have to obey the laws and keep the traditions.

שֶׁאֵינוֹ יוֹדֵעַ לִשְׁאֹל

The Child Who Doesn't Know How To Ask / *Sheh-eino Yodei'ah Li-sh'ol*

Don't bother with questions for this child, just start telling the story: Long ago and far away…

n the land of Ur (1) Abraham lived happily with his wife, Sarah, and their household. One day God spoke to Abraham and told him to move to a new home. God made a promise to Abraham that his descendents would be as numerous as the stars in the sky and protected from danger. It was an offer Abraham couldn't refuse. He packed up his family and belongings and moved to Canaan (2), now known as the land of Israel, where his family grew and prospered. Abraham had a son named Isaac and Isaac had Jacob, who was also called Israel. Jacob-Israel had twelve sons and they became known as the Twelve Tribes of Israel. Of the twelve sons, Jacob's favorite was Joseph.

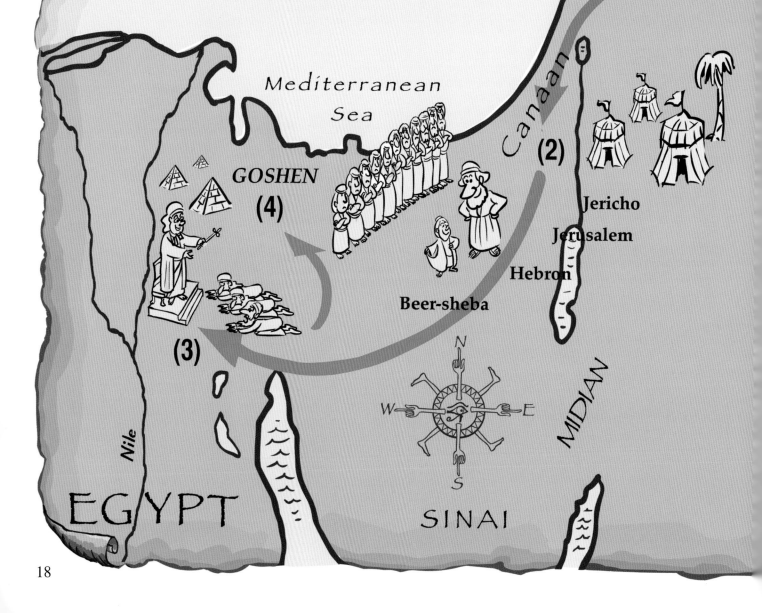

Mediterranean Sea

Canaan

GOSHEN
(4)

(2)

Jericho

Jerusalem

Hebron

Beer-sheba

(3)

N

W   E

S

MIDIAN

Nile

EGYPT

SINAI

KEDAR

Euphrates

BABYLONIA

Babylon

When Jacob gave Joseph presents - such as a splendid colorful robe - his jealous brothers hated him. They sold him into slavery and told their father that Joseph died. One year, a terrible famine struck Canaan and all the countries around it. Crops didn't grow, cattle and people starved and the situation became desperate. In Egypt, though, you could still buy food. So Jacob's sons journeyed to the Nile country (3) seeking relief.

(1)

Ur

In Egypt, the brothers discovered that Joseph was no longer a slave. He had risen from slavery and become the most powerful minister in the land, an adviser to Pharaoh. He was in charge of getting Egypt through the famine. Joseph forgave his brothers for what they had done to him and provided them with food. Jacob, too, came down to Egypt and the whole tribe settled there with their families in an area called Goshen (4).

There were seventy of them and they meant to stay only a short time, but they settled down, raised children there and prospered greatly. Over many generations, the family grew until it became a nation of tens of thousands and it continued to grow until…

ARABIA

One day, a new Pharaoh came to sit on the throne. He feared the growing strength of the Israelites. To get rid of them, he devised a cruel plan: He would make them slaves and work them to death building his great cities. Still, the numbers of Israelites grew.

Frustrated and angry, Pharaoh ordered his men to, "Drown every Israelite newborn son in the river Nile."

On that day, a boy was born to Amram and Yocheved. He had a brother named Aaron and sister Miriam.

His parents kept him out of sight, but after three months, when they could no longer hide him, they wrapped him in a warm blanket and snuck him past Pharaoh's men.

They set the baby afloat on the Nile in a basket made of bulrushes. They hoped someone would take pity on their child and save him. Miriam hid nearby to see what would happen.

At sunrise, Pharaoh's daughter came to bathe in the river and she and her maidens saw the basket. "Look, a baby crying!" she called out. "It must be a Hebrew child."

She took pity on him and let Miriam bring an Israelite woman, who was in fact the child's mother, to nurse him.

Later, Pharaoh's daughter adopted the boy and named him Moses, which means "drawn from the water."

One day, when Moses was grown, he went out from Pharaoh's palace and saw an Egyptian beating someone. It was a fellow Israelite.

Moses struck down the Egyptian and buried him in the sand. He thought there were no witnesses.

The next day he tried to stop a fight between two Israelites. "You're judge and jury now?" one of them asked. "Are you going to kill us the way you killed the Egyptian?" "Uh-oh," thought Moses. "Everyone knows what I've done, probably even the Pharoah." (Gulp!)

Moses fled into the wilderness to the land of Midian.

There he settled, married, had two sons and tended sheep. But he was a stranger in a strange land.

One day, while out with his flock, he came upon an amazing sight: a bush that blazed but wasn't burnt. As he crept closer to get a better look...

God's voice called out from the fire.

"I am sending you to Pharaoh to free my people, the Israelites."

"Me!?!"

"YOU!"

So Moses took his family and returned to Egypt.

22

Pharaoh wasn't about to lose his precious
slaves just because Moses, or some God he had
never heard of, demanded it. Then God told Moses to
make it perfectly clear to Pharaoh that if he didn't let
the Israelites go, the Egyptians would be attacked
by the ten most terrible plagues ever.
And Pharaoh would be to blame. But hard-hearted
Pharaoh dismissed this warning with contempt.

Let My People Go

When Israel was in Egypt's Land,
Let my people go,
Oppressed so hard they could not stand,
Let my people go.

CHORUS
Go down Moses
Way down in Egypt land
Tell ol' Pharaoh
Let my people go!

As Israel stood by the waterside,
Let my people go,
At God's command it did divide,
Let my people go.

CHORUS

Pharaoh said he'd go across,
Let my people go,
But Pharaoh and his host were lost,
Let my people go.

CHORUS

We need not always weep and mourn,
Let my people go,
And wear these slavery chains forlorn,
Let my people go.

CHORUS

As we say each plague's name, we dip a finger in our wine and splash a drop on our plates. It reminds us that no evil deed goes unpunished. Just don't stick your finger in someone else's cup.

BLOOD
Dam דָּם

FROGS
Tzfardei-ah צְפַרְדֵּעַ

LICE
Kinim כִּנִּים

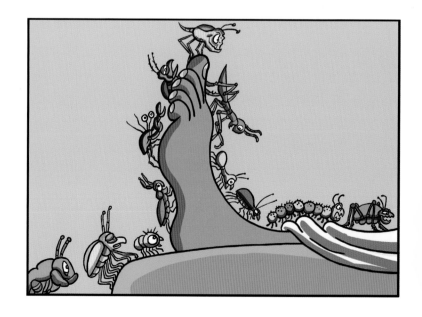

24

WILD BEASTS
Arov עָרוֹב

ANIMAL DISEASE
Dever דֶּבֶר

BOILS
Shechin שְׁחִין

25

HAIL
Barad בָּרָד

LOCUSTS
Arbeh אַרְבֶּה

DARKNESS
Choshekh חֹשֶׁךְ

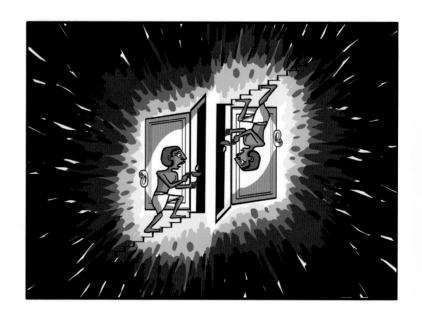

DEATH OF THE FIRSTBORN / *Makat Bekhorot*
מַכַּת בְּכוֹרוֹת

The Israelites didn't have to be told twice.
They got out as fast as their sandals could take them.

The Jews hardly had time to pack food and grab their matzah. It's a good thing they acted so quickly because, just as quickly, Pharaoh had a change of heart. "What have we done? Are we crazy? I want my slaves back!" he said, and the next day he went after them with a great army in chariots. The Egyptians almost caught up with them at the Red Sea. With the sea before them and Pharaoh and his army behind them, the Israelites were trapped.

THE AFI-KOMEN IS NOT HERE.

It was then that a great miracle happened. God caused a strong wind to blow all night and turned the sea into dry land. The water stood like walls as the Israelites passed between them safely. But when the Egyptians charged after them, the walls of water came crashing down and Pharaoh's army drowned. The Israelites were saved.

ven one miracle would have been Dayeinu - "enough for us." But there were so many that we have to sing Dayeinu.

Dayeinu.

דַּיֵּנוּ

If God had only taken us out of Egypt, and not punished the Egyptians Dayeinu...
Chorus: Da-Da-yeinu. Da-Da-yeinu. Da-Da-yeinu. Da-yeinu. Da-yeinu.

If God had only punished the Egyptians and not destroyed their idols Dayeinu...
Da-Da-yeinu. Da-Da-yeinu. Da-Da-yeinu. Da-yeinu. Da-yeinu.

If God had only divided the sea and not led us across dry land Dayeinu...
Da-Da-yeinu. Da-Da-yeinu. Da-Da-yeinu. Da-yeinu. Da-yeinu.

If God had only led us across dry land and not drowned the Egyptians Dayeinu...
Da-Da-yeinu. Da-Da-yeinu. Da-Da-yeinu. Da-yeinu. Da-yeinu.

If God had only given us the Torah and not brought us to the land of Israel Dayeinu...
Da-Da-yeinu. Da-Da-yeinu. Da-Da-yeinu. Da-yeinu. Da-yeinu.

If God had only brought us to the land of Israel and not built the Holy Temple Dayeinu...
Da-Da-yeinu. Da-Da-yeinu. Da-Da-yeinu. Da-yeinu. Da-yeinu.

That's enough for us but you can add more lines like:

If we had only shared this Seder with our family and not with our wonderful guests Dayeinu...
Da-Da-yeinu. Da-Da-yeinu. Da-Da-yeinu. Da-yeinu. Da-yeinu.

That's the end of the story, but not the end of the Seder. It's time for more blessings and rituals before we get to our festive meal. Think of them as Passover appetizers. This may seem needlessly complicated but be patient, as we've been for countless generations. Relax a little more in your chair and fill the second cup of wine. Make the blessing over the wine and drink.

בָּרוּךְ אַתָּה יְיָ, אֱלֹהֵינוּ מֶלֶךְ הָעוֹלָם,
בּוֹרֵא פְּרִי הַגָּפֶן.

Barukh Ata Adonai, Eloheinu
Melekh ha-olam, borei pri ha-gaffen

Blessed are You, our God,
Ruler of the Universe,
Creator of the fruit of the vine.

Washing Hands / *Rochtzah*

רָחְצָה

Wash your hands again in case you
missed anything, and this time make a blessing.

בָּרוּךְ אַתָּה יְיָ, אֱלֹהֵינוּ מֶלֶךְ הָעוֹלָם,
אֲשֶׁר קִדְּשָׁנוּ בְּמִצְוֹתָיו וְצִוָּנוּ עַל נְטִילַת יָדָיִם.

Barukh Ata Adonai, Eloheinu Melekh ha-olam, asher
kideshanu be-mitzvotav ve-tzivanu al netilat yadayim.

Blessed are You, our God, Ruler
of the Universe, Who sanctifies us with
commandments and commands us to wash our hands.

When our ancestors fled Egypt, they couldn't wait for their bread to rise and then bake it in ovens. They threw flat, unleavened dough on a pan over an open fire and made the original fast food that we call matzah. Break the other half of the Afikoman matzah into pieces and pass them around to everyone. Unlike all other nights, we make two blessings before eating the matzah.

Blessing for Matzah / *Motzi Matzah*

מוֹצִיא מַצָּה

בָּרוּךְ אַתָּה יְיָ, אֱלֹהֵינוּ מֶלֶךְ הָעוֹלָם,
הַמּוֹצִיא לֶחֶם מִן הָאָרֶץ.

Barukh Ata Adonai, Eloheinu
Melekh ha-olam, ha-motzi lechem min ha-aretz.

Blessed are You, our God, Ruler of the Universe, Who brings forth bread from the earth.

בָּרוּךְ אַתָּה יְיָ, אֱלֹהֵינוּ מֶלֶךְ הָעוֹלָם,
אֲשֶׁר קִדְּשָׁנוּ בְּמִצְוֹתָיו, וְצִוָּנוּ עַל אֲכִילַת מַצָּה.

Barukh Ata Adonai, Eloheinu Melekh ha-olam, asher kideshanu be-mitzvotav ve-tzivanu al akhilat matzah.

Blessed are You, our God, Ruler of the Universe, Who sanctifies us with commandments and commands us to eat matzah.

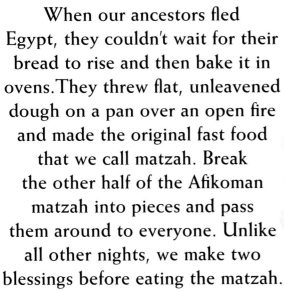

Bitter Herbs / *Maror*

מָרוֹר

The maror (bitter herbs) gives us a taste of what the Israelites suffered in slavery. The charoset looks like the mortar and mud they used to make the heavy bricks for Pharaoh's cities (but it tastes much better). Say the blessing and eat a little maror and charoset together.

בָּרוּךְ אַתָּה יְיָ, אֱלֹהֵינוּ מֶלֶךְ הָעוֹלָם,
אֲשֶׁר קִדְּשָׁנוּ בְּמִצְוֹתָיו וְצִוָּנוּ עַל אֲכִילַת מָרוֹר.

Barukh Ata Adonai, Eloheinu Melekh ha-olam,
asher kideshanu be-mitzvotav ve-tzivanu al akhilat maror.

Blessed are You, our God, Ruler of the Universe, Who sanctifies us with commandments and commands us to eat maror.

Sandwich / *Korekh*

כּוֹרֵךְ

Rabbi Hillel, the great teacher, put maror between two pieces of matzah and invented the "Hillel sandwich." You can add a piece of chazeret (lettuce) for compassion. The sandwich reminds us of the Temple, the bitter times after its destruction and the better times that are coming.

It's also traditional to eat a hard-boiled egg
(like the one on the Seder Plate) with a little parsley.
It symbolizes the celebration of life and the rebirth of spring.

The shank bone on the
Seder Plate is for the strong
arm of God that brought us out of
bondage. But we don't eat it.

Festive Meal / *Shulchan Orekh*

שֻׁלְחָן עוֹרֵךְ

The table is spread and ready.
Finally, we're free.

Let's eat!

Hidden Dessert / *Tzafun* צָפוּן

After the meal, get ready to find the Afikoman.
Look under the rug and behind the cabinet. It can't have gone
too far considering a matzah's legs aren't very long.

Blessing after Meal / *Barekh* בָּרֵךְ

We raise the third cup of wine, but don't drink it,
and say Grace after the Meal, the short version.

"Blessed are You Adonai our God, Ruler of the Universe, Who provides food
for the world. Your kindness lasts forever. For You are God who feeds and cares
for everyone, and does good for all that You have created."

Settling ever deeper in our chairs, we
make a blessing over the wine and drink the third cup.

בָּרוּךְ אַתָּה יְיָ, אֱלֹהֵינוּ מֶלֶךְ הָעוֹלָם,
בּוֹרֵא פְּרִי הַגָּפֶן.

Barukh Ata Adonai, Eloheinu Melekh ha-olam, borei pri ha-gaffen.

Blessed are You, our God, Ruler of the Universe,
Creator of the fruit of the vine.

As for that special wine goblet, that's for Elijah the Prophet. He was just here. Didn't you see him? He went in and out through the door we opened. Check the cup. It's not as full as it was before. He brought a message of justice and peace, reminding us that there are still many people who are oppressed by tyrants today.

Praising God / *Hallel*

הַלֵּל

Hallel is the song of praise and celebration for the Israelites' deliverance. Like Miriam the prophetess and all the Israelite women who sang with timbrels and danced, we also lift our voices in joy and gratitude:

"Sing ye to the Lord, for He is highly exalted:
The horse and his rider hath He thrown into the sea."

Chad Gadya

 Chad gadya, Chad gadya.

My father bought for two zuzim.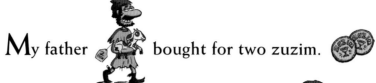

Then came the cat and ate the my  bought for

Then came the dog and bit the that

ate the  my bought for

Then came the stick 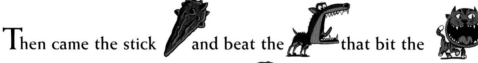 and beat the that bit the

that ate the  my bought for

Then came the fire and burned the that beat the

that bit the that ate the  my bought for

Then came the water and quenched the that burned

the that beat the  that bit the that ate

the  my bought for

Then came the ox and drank the that quenched the that burned the that beat the that bit the that ate the my bought for

Then came the butcher and slew the that drank the that quenched the that burned the that beat the that bit the that ate the my bought for

Then came the angel of death and killed the that slew the that drank the that quenched the that burned the that beat the that bit the that ate the my bought for

Then came the Blessed Holy One and destroyed the that killed the that slew the that drank the that quenched the that burned the that beat the that bit the that ate the my bought for

Chad gadya, Chad gadya.

WHO KNOWS ONE ? / ECHAD MI YODEA?

The traditional wake-up-after-dinner-sing-a-long.
1. The leader sings "One. Who knows one?" The first person to the right answers "One? I know one! One is our God, Who is in heaven and on earth."
2. Everyone sings the chorus, pointing up on the word *shamayim* and pointing down on *aretz*.
3. The leader sings "Two. Who knows two?" The second person to the right sings "Two? I know two! Two are the tablets of the covenant." The first person repeats the first answer. Everyone sings the chorus again and so it goes faster and faster around the table. You lose your breath and you'll lose your turn.

1
Who knows one?
One? I know one!

One is our God, Who is in heaven and on earth.

Chorus: *Echad Eloheinu, Eloheinu, Eloheinu, Eloheinu she-ba-shamayim u-va-aretz*

2
Who knows two?
Two? I know two!

Two are the tablets of the covenant.
One is our God, Who is in heaven and on earth.

3
Who knows three?
Three? I know three!

Three are the patriarchs.
Two are the tablets of the covenant.
One is our God, Who is in heaven and on earth.

4
Who knows four?
Four? I know four!

Four are the matriarchs.
Three are the patriarchs.
Two are the tablets of the covenant.
One is our God, Who is in heaven and on earth.

5

Who knows five?
Five? I know five!

Five are the books of the Torah.
Four are the matriarchs.
Three are the patriarchs.
Two are the tablets of the covenant.
One is our God, Who is in heaven and on earth.

6

Who knows six?
Six? I know six!

Six are the sections of the Mishnah.
Five are the books of the Torah.
Four are the matriarchs.
Three are the patriarchs.
Two are the tablets of the covenant.
One is our God, Who is in heaven and on earth

7

Who knows seven?
Seven? I know seven!

Seven are the days of the week.
Six are the sections of the Mishnah.
Five are the books of the Torah.
Four are the matriarchs.
Three are the patriarchs.
Two are the tablets of the covenant.
One is our God, Who is in heaven and on earth.

8

Who knows eight?
Eight? I know eight!

Eight are the days before circumcision.
Seven are the days of the week.
Six are the sections of the Mishnah.
Five are the books of the Torah.
Four are the matriarchs.
Three are the patriarchs.
Two are the tablets of the covenant.
One is our God, Who is in heaven and on earth.

9

Who knows nine?
Nine? I know nine!

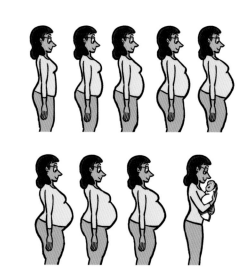

Nine are the months of childbirth.
Eight are the days before circumcision.
Seven are the days of the week.
Six are the sections of the Mishnah.
Five are the books of the Torah.
Four are the matriarchs.
Three are the patriarchs.
Two are the tablets of the covenant.
One is our God, Who is in heaven and on earth.

10

Who knows ten?
Ten? I know ten!

Ten are the commandments.
Nine are the months of childbirth.
Eight are the days before circumcision.
Seven are the days of the week.
Six are the sections of the Mishnah.
Five are the books of the Torah.
Four are the matriarchs.
Three are the patriarchs.
Two are the tablets of the covenant.
One is our God, Who is in heaven and on earth.

11

Who knows eleven?
Eleven? I know eleven!

Eleven are the stars in Joseph's dream.
Ten are the commandments.
Nine are the months of childbirth.
Eight are the days before circumcision.
Seven are the days of the week.
Six are the sections of the Mishnah.
Five are the books of the Torah.
Four are the matriarchs.
Three are the patriarchs.
Two are the tablets of the covenant.
One is our God, Who is in heaven and on earth.

12

Who knows twelve?
Twelve? I know twelve!

Twelve are the tribes of Israel.
Eleven are the stars in Joseph's dream.
Ten are the commandments.
Nine are the months of childbirth.
Eight are the days before circumcision.
Seven are the days of the week.
Six are the sections of the Mishnah.
Five are the books of the Torah.
Four are the matriarchs.
Three are the patriarchs.
Two are the tablets of the covenant.
One is our God, Who is in heaven and on earth.

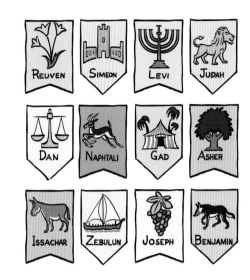

13

Who knows thirteen?
Thirteen? I know thirteen!

Thirteen are God's attributes.
Twelve are the tribes of Israel.
Eleven are the stars in Joseph's dream.
Ten are the commandments.
Nine are the months of childbirth.
Eight are the days before circumcision.
Seven are the days of the week.
Six are the sections of the Mishnah.
Five are the books of the Torah.
Four are the matriarchs.
Three are the patriarchs.
Two are the tablets of the covenant.
One is our God, Who is in heaven and on earth.

Raise your fourth cup of wine and repeat the blessing.

בָּרוּךְ אַתָּה יְיָ, אֱלֹהֵינוּ מֶלֶךְ הָעוֹלָם,
בּוֹרֵא פְּרִי הַגָּפֶן.

Barukh Ata Adonai, Eloheinu Melekh ha-olam, borei pri ha-gaffen.

**Blessed are You, our God, Ruler
of the Universe, Creator of the fruit of the vine.**

Conclusion / *Nirtzah*

נִרְצָה

hat's it for tonight. The Seder is done.
Together we relaxed, drank, asked questions, told
stories, ate and sang. To end our celebration, we say,
aloud, all together, as Jews have done all over the
world for thousands of years:

Next Year in Jerusalem!

לְשָׁנָה הַבָּאָה בִּירוּשָׁלָיִם!

Recipes:

Classic Charoset (serving 6)

Even though charoset symbolizes the bricks and mortar
of our ancestors' slavery, it doesn't have to taste like mud.

Ingredients:
3 green cooking apples,
cored and quartered
3 tablespoons honey or to taste
1 tablespoon lemon juice

Optional:
raisins
chopped almonds, pecans or walnuts
dates, pitted and chopped
1/2 teaspoon cinnamon
2 tablespoons red wine or orange juice

In a food processor, grate apples into medium to coarse
chunks. Stir in lemon juice to preserve color and mix in honey.
Pour into large bowl and add the optional ingredients.
Cover and refrigerate at least three hours.

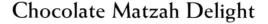

Chocolate Matzah Delight

If the Israelites had dessert before they left Egypt,
this is it. Go easy on the liqueur.

Ingredients:
6 matzahs, finely crumbled (1/4-inch bits)
6 ounces semisweet cooking chocolate
1/4 cup water
3 tablespoons honey
3 tablespoons sugar
3 tablespoons margarine
sweetened cocoa powder
sweetened coconut flakes
1 grated lemon rind
3 tablespoons liqueur (optional)
3 tablespoons coffee (optional)

1. Coat 25 small paper baking cups with a pinch of
coconut flakes or cocoa powder.

2. In a large mixing bowl hand crumble the matzahs.

3. In a small saucepan put water, chocolate, honey, sugar,
margarine and optional ingredients.

4. Place the small saucepan in a larger pan
with 2 inches water and heat.

5. Stir continually with a wooden spoon until the chocolate mixture
is smooth and syrupy. Heat the chocolate without boiling or steaming.

6. Pour the hot mixture over the crumbled matzah till it is completely covered.

7. Fill the cups with the chocolate-covered matzah and gently press it down.

8. Sprinkle with cocoa powder or coconut flakes.
Garnish with blueberries, sliced strawberries or almonds.

9. Refrigerate for at least two hours before serving.

Richard Codor makes a
living drawing humorously.
His work appears in *Hadassah
Magazine* and is featured in the
books *All You Want To Know About
Sabbath Services* (**Behrman House**),
The Big Book of Jewish Humor (**Collins**)
and the Israeli social satire classic,
Zoo Eretz Zoo (E.L.S. Editions).
His secular cartoons and
drawings appear in numerous
multiethnic, politically correct
and incorrect movies,
TV and Internet media.

Liora Codor, artist, photographer,
mother and keeper of traditions,
lives with Richard in Brooklyn, NY.